LONGMAN NATURE LIBRARY

BATS

LONGMAN NATURE LIBRARY

BATS

Longman

Longman Group Limited
Longman House, Burnt Mill, Harlow,
Essex CM20 2JE, England
and Associated Companies throughout the world.

First published 1985

British Library Cataloguing in Publication Data
Bats. — (Longman nature library)
1. Bats
599.4 QL737.C5

ISBN 0-582-89263-5

Edited and designed by Curtis Garratt Limited
The Old Vicarage, Horton cum Studley
Oxford OX9 1BT

Index by Barbara James

Set in MCS 9/10 pt Mallard

Printed in Spain
by TONSA, San Sebastian

CONTENTS

INTRODUCTION

There are only two major groups of animals with backbones, or vertebrates, which actually fly under their own power. The best-known of these are certainly the birds, but the other group is mammalian - the bats. The ability to fly has clearly proved to be an advantage because bats represent nearly a quarter of all known species of mammals. Yet, surprisingly, very little, if anything, is known about many of them. There are other animals, such as insects, that can fly. There are also mammals unrelated to bats, such as flying squirrels, that can glide from tree to tree. Insects, birds, and bats have all evolved wings. When unrelated groups of animals develop similar structures as a response to living in similar conditions, the process is known as convergent evolution.

Most people have an idea of what a mammal is, and this idea is probably quite close to the scientific definition. The word 'mammal' is derived from the Latin *mammalis* meaning breast, and mammals are characterized by suckling their young on a nourishing milk produced and secreted by the mammary glands or breasts of the female. Mammals are vertebrates, which are those animals that possess a bony or cartilaginous rod or backbone running along the back side of the trunk of the animal from the head to the tail region. They are often referred to as warm blooded although, more correctly, they should be called homoiothermic; in other words, they are able to maintain their internal body temperature at a more or less constant level regardless of the environmental conditions. In contrast, most animals, other than birds and mammals, are poikilothermic which means that their body temperature varies in response to the environmental conditions.

Because they need to maintain their body temperatures, the great majority of mammals, including bats, possess a layer of hair which insulates the body, as does the covering of feathers on a bird. Mammals also usually have sweat glands in their skin which enable them to cool their bodies by sweating in hot conditions. Mammals are usually considered to be intelligent and, although intelligence may not be directly related to brain size, they do have relatively large brains. They do not lay eggs, as birds and reptiles do, but they give birth to comparatively well-developed offspring which are then reared on the mother's milk.

Most of these characteristics, together with the typical four-footed method of locomotion and socketed teeth in the jaws, are ideally fitted to a life on land where the mammals first evolved. Flying, especially at night as most bats do, clearly presents a different set of requirements. To be able to fly, an animal needs wings, but the wings of bats are quite different from those of birds. They possess a double flap or membrane of hairless skin which stretches from between the forearm and elongated fingers of each forelimb to the hind limbs, sometimes including the tail. The upper part of each arm is quite short, and the thumb is reduced to a short claw which projects beyond the leading edge of the wing. These claws are used to help the animal cling to surfaces and to move, especially when it is at the roosting site.

The bones of the hand form the main part of the framework for the wing so it is hardly surprising that the scientific name for bats, Chiroptera, means 'hand winged'. Most bats are unable to fly very rapidly but they can manoeuvre with remarkable agility. Indeed, bats are so well adapted for flying that their limbs can scarcely support their weight when they are on the ground and they move very awkwardly. Thus, they hang upside down to roost and have only to let go and spread their wings to take flight.

Most birds fly and feed during the day so that they have excellent eyesight, only moderate hearing, and a poor sense of smell. The majority of bats, on the other hand, are nocturnal so that, although fruit bats, for example, have good eyesight, most other bats rely on a different means to navigate around obstacles and to pinpoint their food in the darkness. Rather like many of the sea mammals, they use a combination of superb hearing and a system of echolocation which works on the same principle as radar. Alhough bats have eyes, they can still fly, feed, and manoeuvre even if they have been blinded. Bats produce pulses of sound, which are usually beyond the range of human hearing. The sounds are emitted through the mouth or, in some bats, through the nose. They bounce back off any object which they encounter and are picked up by the animal's acute hearing, enabling the bat to navigate with astonishing accuracy. It is unlikely that a bat will get tangled in someone's hair - a popular myth.

Classification of bats

There are two main groups of bats. The fruit bats, otherwise known as flying foxes, include the largest of all the bats and, as one of their common names suggests, they have large eyes and rather fox-like faces. There are less than 200 different kinds of these bats found throughout much of the Old World while all the rest of the 700 or so types of bats are included in the remaining major group. They are found in a wide variety of different habitats throughout much of the world except for the arctic and Antarctica. This book describes representatives of both groups of bats.

There is a bewildering array of living things occupying planet Earth and, for a better understanding of the living world, scientists have found it convenient to divide this wealth of life into different groups of various sizes. The process by which these scientists, known as taxonomists, classify animals and plants is a complex and exacting one, requiring detailed knowledge of the anatomy, physiology, ecology, evolutionary history, and relationships of the life forms. As more and more is discovered about the natural world, the classification of living things must be constantly modified. It was once thought that all life forms could simply be divided into two kingdoms - animals and plants. Most modern systems, however, suggest that there may be as many as five kingdoms. These divisions are decided upon the basis of many factors, such as the levels of organization of the creature or plant and the various ways in which it feeds and provides itself with energy for growth, maintenance, and reproduction. Whatever system is used, though, an animal kingdom is always recognized, and this can be our starting point when we look at the different types of flying mammals, or bats, which are the subject of this book.

The animal kingdom is divided into a number of major groups called 'phyla' (singular 'phylum'). The phylum known as Chordata contains all the animals,

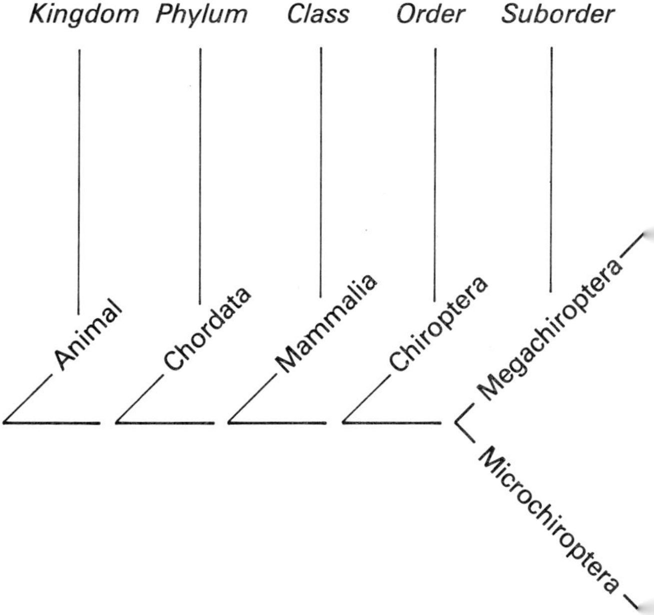

Classification of Bats

Family

Pteropodidae – fruit bats

Rhinopomatidae – mouse-tailed bats
Emballonuridae – sheath-tailed bats
Craseonycteridae – hog-nosed bats
Nycteridae – slit-faced bats
Megadermatidae – false vampires
Rhinolophidae – horseshoe bats
Hipposideridae – Old World leaf-nosed bats
Noctilionidae – fisherman bats
Mormoopidae – moustached bats
Desmodontidae – vampire bats
Molossidae – free-tailed bats
Phyllostomatidae – New World leaf-nosed bats
Vespertilionidae – evening bats
Natalidae – funnel-eared bats
Furipteridae – smoky bats
Thyropteridae – disc-winged bats
Myzopodidae – sucker-footed bats
Mystacinidae – New Zealand short-tailed bats

such as fishes, amphibians, birds, reptiles, and mammals, that are characterized by possessing a flexible supporting rod in the body at some stage of their life. We have already described the major features of animals which are recognized as mammals and which are, therefore, included in the 'class' Mammalia. The mammals are further divided into a number of 'orders', such as the Chiroptera (bats), and each order contains a number of 'families'. For example, all the flying foxes are included in the family Pteropodidae while the sixty-nine species of horseshoe bats make up the family Rhinolophidae. In this book, we shall be considering all nineteen families of bats.

People often wonder why taxonomists have to give things seemingly difficult names consisting of two latinized words, conventionally printed in italics. For example, why should a common pipistrelle be called *Pipistrellus pipistrellus* rather than simply a common pipistrelle or even flying mouse - another of its colloquial names? In the eighteenth century, it was the intention of the Swedish naturalist, Carolus Linnaeus to give every living thing a unique scientific name to avoid confusion. It is on his original work that our present system is based. For example, the animal which is commonly known in English as the common flying fox is certainly not a fox, or even closely related to one. It actually belongs to the family Pteropodidae and is, therefore, a fruit bat. Of course, it has other common names in different languages but internationally it is known as *Pteropus vampyrus*. These two words also give an indication of the origins, form, and relationships of this animal.

Looking at the scientific name, the fruit bats included in the family Pteropodidae, such as the common flying fox or the Indian flying fox, both belong to the 'genus' *Pteropus* but only the common flying fox or common fruit bat, which is a clearly separate 'species' is called *Pteropus vampyrus*. The word *'vampyrus'* is the species name and it is the species which is the basic unit of classification. That which constitutes a species is largely beyond the scope of this book but one simple definition is that a species is a population of living things which do not differ from one another fundamentally, which do differ from members of other species, and which are able to breed among themselves to produce fertile offspring. To give an example: there is a number of different kinds of fruit bat which belong to the genus *Pteropus* but only one common flying fox which is different in many respects from *Pteropus rodricensis*, the Rodriguez fruit bat, and, indeed, from the other fruit bats.

Evolution of bats

Over the vast aeons of geological time, many different species of living things have appeared and disappeared in response to changes in their environment. It is generally accepted that new species evolve as a result of natural selection. By this process, organisms which are well fitted to their environment tend to survive and breed more successfully than those which are less well adapted, thereby increasing the proportion of their offspring in the next generation. In turn, they will form a distinct group and eventually a new species will emerge.

When did the first bats appear on our planet and what were the pressures that drove them into the air and to a nocturnal way of life? Like their life styles today, the evolutionary history of bats is not well known because few fossil remains of early bats have ever been found. The oldest known fossil was found in rocks that are some 50 million years old. Until the end of the Cretaceous period of the Earth's history, some 64 million years ago, it was reptiles and, in particular, the dinosaurs which dominated the land-dwelling animals inhabiting the Earth. At that point, and for reasons which are still a matter of heated debate, the age of the dinosaurs came to an abrupt end. Mammals had existed but, because of the dinosaur's dominance during the daytime, most of them were small, skulking, night-active creatures. With the dinosaur's reign over, mammals began to flourish, spreading into a wide range of new habitats.

The reason why birds first took to the air is also not fully understood but, clearly, this ability enabled them to escape from earthbound predators as well as exploiting new food sources, such as flying insects, which would not have been available to ground-dwelling animals. And so it was, perhaps, with the bats. In addition, their ability to fly has enabled bats to colonize areas, such as oceanic islands, which are largely denied to many other mammals. For example, on Mahe, the principal island of the Seychelles group, there are only three species of native mammals - and all of them are bats! In fact, the meat of the Seychelles fruit bat is a local delicacy.

Food and feeding

All animals need to find enough food of the right kind to be able to live, grow, and reproduce, otherwise individuals and eventually the species would die out.

Bats occupy most habitats and feed on a wide variety of food items. Myths and legends have told much of the legendary vampire bat but, far from being one of the forms of Count Dracula draining the life blood from human victims, it feeds almost entirely on the blood from just a single breed of cattle.

Ranging in weight from as little as 1.5 grams to 1.5 kilograms, bats feed on a wide variety of food items including insects, other invertebrates, small mammals, reptiles and amphibians, fishes, fruit, and other plant material. Indeeed, some bats are important pollinators of plants and, where their numbers have been reduced either by hunting or destruction of habitat, the plants, too, suffer as a result.

Habitat and distribution

Bats were originally largely tropical mammals but they are now distributed widely throughout most of the tropical and temperate regions of the world. Consequently, like a number of animals living in cooler climes, many of them are obliged to hibernate in times of severe weather when food is scarce. They find a variety of sites, including buildings, mineshafts, trees, and, of course, caves, often huddling together in very large numbers to conserve heat.

Courtship and mating

The reproductive behaviour of bats seems to be closely linked with available food supplies although, once again, the breeding biology for most species is not well known. They probably mate at the roost sites and, in some species, implantation of the fertilized egg is delayed. Bats probably do not form pair bonds, as such, and they probably mate indiscriminately with more than one individual. Usually only a single offspring is born, perhaps once a year. It is interesting to note that, in many species, the young is born while the mother is hanging upside down which presents some very special problems for birth. The offspring is usually suckled by its mother until it is able to become independent.

Conservation of bats

Bats are just one more group of animals that is suffering at the hands of human intervention in the balance of nature. Despite the fact that bats are now fully protected throughout Europe, as well as in many other countries, their numbers are everywhere declining and some have already become extinct. Island populations, in particular, have suffered as their traditional forests have been felled to make way for agricultural land to feed the increasing populations. And, in most places, it is destruction of habitat that is leading to the demise of bats as it is for so many other animals. But the larger species are also a source of meat so they are often hunted in greater numbers now than they have been in the past. And, of course, because they are little-known night fliers, they have long been associated with the devil and other mythical evils. It is sometimes hard to understand why such small, largely inoffensive creatures have provoked so much fear among humans but, in some parts of the world, such as the United States, it has led to them being regarded as pests and eradicated in large numbers from homes and other buildings. It is to be hoped that, as our knowledge of the habits of bats improves, and people in general become more willing to accept their presence, no more species will be lost, never to return.

ABOUT THIS BOOK

There are some 4000 species of mammals distributed around the world, ranging from the tiniest shrews to the massive blue whale. Of these, around 950 species are bats, representing nearly a quarter of the world's mammals. Few books, therefore, can hope to be comprehensive not least because the biologies of many of these bats are little known and, in some cases, the bats have been observed only a few times.

Bats has been designed to describe and illustrate a small but representative selection of these fascinating but little-known mammals to show their diverse range of sizes, forms, lifestyles, and distribution. It has not, of course, been possible to include all 950 species of bats but, in this one small volume, but at least one member from each of the nineteen families has been described and, in the case of the larger and more important families, such as the evening bats, a sensible selection has been made.

This is not a field guide but, using the fine illustrations and concise but authoritative descriptions in tandem, it should be possible to decide to which family a bat belongs if you are ever lucky enough to have the chance to see one. In addition, if you read through the book, it will give you a good general catalogue of the various types of bats that range most of the world.

Fruit Bats

SUBORDER MEGACHIROPTERA

The bats are divided into two major groups, or suborders. (The major groups used in the classification of animals and plants are defined in the introduction. Any of these groups, however, can be divided into 'subgroups' or lumped together into 'supergroups'.) These are the Megachiroptera, or 'big hand wings' and the Microchiroptera or 'small hand wings'. The fruit bats or flying foxes belong to the Megachiroptera which contains a single family, the Pteropodidae, with some 173 species in forty-four genera.

As their two common names suggest, were it not for their wings, they would appear distinctly fox-like (some even have red-coloured fur), and they feed mainly on fruit and other plant material, including pollen, nectar, and even leaves when food is short. Some species will also eat insects. The body length ranges from as little as 5 centimetres (2 inches) to as much as 45 centimetres (18 inches), with wing spans of up to 1.5 or even 2 metres (5 to 6.6 feet). Flying by day in large numbers, as they sometimes do, they make an impressive sight and their flapping wings can make a quite audible whistling sound.

Fruit bats have large eyes, giving them excellent vision, and relatively small, widely set ears. They seem to have a highly developed sense of smell. Apparently, some species have a poorly developed echolocation system which perhaps functions as a navigational aid in finding their roosting sites. Hanging from their tree roosts, some species look like huge dangling fruits themselves. The claw on the first 'finger' is strong, well developed and hook like, and some species have an extra claw on the second 'finger' at the leading edge of the wings. Using these claws, together with their feet, they manoeuvre along the branches of trees in search of their food.

Fruit bats live mainly in the tropical and subtropical parts of the Old World, from Africa to eastern Asia and Australia, including many of the islands of the Pacific and the Indian Ocean. Some species are extremely rare. For example, the Rodriguez fruit bat, has been reduced in numbers to as few as 200 individuals in the wild state. Possibly in the nick of time, however, the Rodriguez fruit bat has been the subject of a major rescue operation by Gerald Durrell and his team and there is now a thriving population in captivity at the Jersey Zoo. Because many of the animals are relatively large, they have been traditionally hunted for food with no serious effects on their populations but, with the advent of guns and continued destruction of their forest habitats, their numbers have dwindled dramatically in recent years. They are still eaten in some parts of the world, such as the Seychelles, but there at least it is forbidden to use firearms for hunting them - indeed, on those islands, firearms are very strictly controlled. The flesh of a fruit bat tastes rather like that of rabbit but is even bonier and hardly makes for substantial eating.

Fruit Bats

The greater or Indian fruit bat inhabits the forest and scrub areas of southern and south-eastern Asia, where it can be found roosting in trees during the day in flocks of many thousands. The flocks usually use the same roosts throughout the year. At dusk, they fly out in search of their food. It is thought that they rely mainly on the juice of fruit for nourishment, crushing the fruit with their peg-like teeth and spitting out the flesh and pips. Bananas, on the other hand, may be swallowed whole.

Living as they do in the tropics, greater fruit bats may give birth to their single offspring at most times of the year, although in any particular area, births occur at more or less the same time. It takes about six months from conception for the young to be born and it is then carried by its mother for a further two months but it may be up to three months after it is born before its is able to make its first flight.

Suborder Megachiroptera - fruit bats (about 170 species)

Family/Species Pteropodidae - fruit bats or flying foxes (about 170 species)/Greater Fruit Bat (Indian Flying Fox) *Pteropus giganteus*

Length 35-40 cm (14-16 in)

Hammerheaded Bat

The curious-looking hammerheaded bat is found only in the tropical forests, mangrove swamps, and other swampy areas of Africa from The Gambia to Uganda and Angola. In most fruit bats, the males and females are similar but, in this case, the mature males develop an extraordinary nasal swelling, which gives the species its name, as well as a huge bony larynx. The male is almost twice as large as the female. The function of the nasal apparatus of this bat was once a mystery but it is now thought to play an important part in the breeding biology of the animal and is involved in the male's territorial display.

Unlike most mammals, hammerheaded bats, adopt a lek system rather like that of certain birds such as the capercaillie. The males gather at the lek site during the two annual dry seasons and give voice to metallic-sounding calls. Mature males may even fight for the best territories at the site. The females then choose their partners and mating takes place. The single offspring is born after a gestation period of about five or six months and looks after her baby without any help from the male.

It has been suggested that hammerheaded bats may be carnivorous but it is now thought that they live entirely on a diet of fruit, especially ripe figs as well as mangoes and other fruits.

Suborder Megachiroptera - fruit bats (about 170 species)
Family/Species Pteropodidae - fruit bats or flying foxes (about 170 species)/Hammerheaded Bat *Hypsignathus monstrosus*
Length 25-30 cm (10-12 in)

Dog Bat

Unlike most other fruit bats, dog bats roost mainly in rock crevices and caves and use audible clicking sounds, which they make with their tongues, as an echolocation device to aid navigation in finding their roosts. They still retain the large eyes typical of the family, however, and, once they have found the entrance to their cave, they rely on their eyesight thereafter. They may roost in vast numbers in these caves or even in tombs and temples. Dog bats live in forested areas from Africa eastwards to India and Malaysia. Unlike the insect-eating bats which commonly use echolocation techniques, dog bats feed mainly on fruit juices, pollen, and nectar and they will fly long distances in search of their food. Because of their feeding habits, they are important pollinators for a number of plant species.

Dog bats breed between December and March and the single offspring is born after a gestation period of about four months. It is suckled by its mother until it is able to feed on fruit at about the age of three months. Until it is able to fly, it clings tightly to its mother and is carried with her wherever she might go.

Suborder Megachiroptera - fruit bats (about 170 species)

Family/Species Pteropodidae - fruit bats or flying foxes (about 170 species)/Dog Bat *Rousettus aegyptiacus*

Length 30-45 cm (12-18 in)

Franquet's Fruit Bat

Franquet's fruit bat lives in the forests and open country of the tropical, mainly central parts of Africa from Nigeria in the west to Angola, and Zimbabwe and Tanzania in the east. Unlike the dog bat, for example, which has a short tail, this fruit bat has no tail but it does have noticeable areas of white fur on each shoulder which give it its alternative name of epauleted fruit bat. Again, unlike most of the other fruit bats, it roosts alone rather than in colonies.

It does feed on the juice of fruit but, instead of crushing the fruit between its teeth and then spitting out the flesh and pips, it holds the fruit between its lips, makes an incision with its teeth, and then sucks out the juice by a pumping action of its throat.

Like many bats which live in tropical, rather than temperate regions, it is able to breed at all times of the year. The single young is born after a gestation period of three to four months.

Order Megachiroptera - fruit bats (about 170 species)
Family/Species Pteropodidae - fruit bats or flying foxes (about 170 species)/Franquet's Fruit Bat (Epauleted Fruit Bat) *Epomops franqueti*
Length 14-18 cm (5.5-7 in)

Harpy Fruit Bat

The harpy fruit bat is a very rare and elusive species, restricted to the Philippines and the island of Celebes or Sulawesi in Indonesia, off the south-east coast of Asia. It inhabits forested areas up to an altitude of some 1700 metres (5600 feet).

Little seems to be known about this tailless species of fruit bat. It has scissor-like incisor teeth which it probably uses to cut from the trees the figs and other fruit upon which it feeds.

Order Megachiroptera - fruit bats (about 170 species)

Family/Species Pteropodidae - fruit bats or flying foxes (about 170 species)/Harpy Fruit Bat *Harpionycteris whiteheadi*

Length 14-15 cm (5.5-6 in)

Tube-nosed Fruit Bat

This fruit bat gets its name from the scroll-like tubes which stand out on either side of its nose. It inhabits the forested areas of the islands of south-east Asia, including Celebes and Timor, as well as the Solomon Islands, Papua New Guinea, and northern Australia. Its yellow speckled wings probably afford it some camouflage while it roosts, usually alone, clinging to the trunks of trees. This species possesses a short tail.

It feeds on the juice of a variety of ripe fruit, including guavas, figs, and the flesh of young coconuts. It is thought possible that the 'nasal scrolls' help it to find its food by giving the animal more ability to locate accurately the direction from which smells are emanating in much the same way as humans use their stereoscopic vision to produce a three-dimensional effect.

Breeding takes place in September and October and a single offspring is born.

Suborder Megachiroptera - fruit bats (about 170 species)

Family/Species Pteropodidae - fruit bats or flying foxes (about 170 species)/Tube-nosed Fruit Bat *Nyctimene major*

Length 8-14 cm (3-5.5 in)

Common Long-tongued Fruit Bat

Although it is a small animal, with its fox-like face, fairly small, simple ears, and large eyes, the common long-tongued fruit bat is, in its superficial appearance, typical of the family. It inhabits the forests and plantations (where it is often considered to be a pest) of the Burmese mainland of south-east Asia, south-east to Malaysia and the island of Bali.

Some animals adopt a strategy of living in large flocks or herds to afford them some protection from their enemies but this bat seems to achieve similar ends by living a very solitary life so that it becomes less noticeable to predators. During the day, it roosts among rolled-up banana or hemp leaves. It sets off at dusk in search of food, its diet consisting of the nectar and pollen of flowers as well as some fruit. At night it frequently gives voice to shrieking calls.

The breeding season occurs during August and September, and the single offspring is born three to four months after conception.

Suborder Megachiroptera - fruit bats (about 170 species)

Family/Species Pteropodidae - fruit bats or flying foxes (about 170 species)/Common Long-tongued Fruit Bat *Macroglossus minimus*

Length 6-7 cm (2.4-2.8 in)

Queensland Blossom Bat

In spite of its name, this fruit bat is not restricted to Queensland, Australia but ranges from southern Papua New Guinea southwards as far as New South Wales where it inhabits both damp and dry acacia and eucalyptus forests. One part of its name, at least, is less misleading for it certainly seems to feed almost entirely on the nectar and pollen from the flowers of acacias which it extracts by probing into the long necks of the blossoms with its brush-like tongue.

It is even smaller than the common long-tongued fruit bat and, indeed, is the smallest member of the family. The tiny offspring is born in November or December.

Suborder Megachiroptera - fruit bats (about 170 species)

Family/Species Pteropodidae - fruit bats or flying foxes (about 170 species)/Queensland Blossom Bat *Syconycteris australis*

Length 5-6 cm (2-2.4 in)

SUBORDER MICROCHIROPTERA

This group includes all bats except for the fruit bats or flying foxes. There are almost 800 species in eighteen (or possibly nineteen) families within the suborder. The group is a world-ranging and diverse collection of flying mammals. It is uncertain whether or not the two suborders of bats evolved from the same ancestor - a small, shrew-like, insect-eating mammal, for instance - or from quite separate lines; it is hard to establish because so few fossil bats have ever been found. One point of interest is that the single member of the hog-nosed bat family may well be the world's smallest mammal, weighing as little as 2 grams. Echolocation is highly developed among the members of this group, and adaptations for sending and receiving signals, such as the nose leaves of the horseshoe bats, are common. Ears tend to be large. Many species feed on insects, usually caught on the wing, but others eat nectar, pollen, fruit, fishes, and small mammals.

As their name suggests, the mouse-tailed bats of Asia are characterized by their naked tails which may be as long as their bodies, while the tail of the tropical and subtropical sheath-tailed bats protrudes through a membrane which stretches between the hind legs. Obviously, the single species in the hog-nosed bat family of Africa and Asia gets its name from its rather pig-like nose. Once again, the slit-faced bats are so called because of the pair of slits which divides their nose leaves and eyes.

False vampire bats prey on other bats but it was once thought that they sucked their blood. The horseshoe bats have a horseshoe-shaped fleshy structure around the nose which is involved with the sounds that they produce through their nostrils. The various species are found throughout the tropical and temperate regions of the Old World. Also of the Old World, the group of leaf-nosed bats have similar nasal structures to the horseshoe bats.

There are two species only of fisherman or bulldog bats and, as their name implies, they feed on fishes and have rather bulldog-like faces.

The eight species of moustached bats have a moustache-like fringe of hair around the nose, and they occupy the southern parts of the United States, southwards to Brazil. The well-known vampire bats are specialized to feed on the blood of animals - often just a single type of cattle. They are found in Central America and there are only three species. The large family of insect-eating free-tailed bats have rat-like tails which project beyond the tail membranes.

Another large family, the leaf-nosed bats of the Americas, also possess the characteristic nose leaves but they are mainly pollen and insect eaters. The evening bat family includes some 300 species, which are mostly small insect eaters, and they are found throughout the world. The origin of the name of the funnel-eared bats of tropical South America is obvious, and the two species of smoky bats are, as their name indicates, smoky in colour. Disc-winged bats have sucker-like pads near the leading and trailing edges of their wings which enable them to climb the trunks of trees. There is just one species of sucker-winged bat, which lives on the island of Madagascar. Finally, the single species of short-tailed bat is one of the very few native mammals of New Zealand.

Greater Mouse-tailed Bat

The greater mouse-tailed bat has, as its name suggests, a slender, mouse-like tail which may be as long as the head and body together. They live in the dry, treeless areas, savannas, and even urban areas of the Middle and Near East. Originally, they roosted in caves but, for thousands of years, they have roosted in great numbers in buildings, particularly temples, palaces, and even pyramids. The ears are connected by a fleshy prominence which extends, across the forehead, from the front of the ear opening. Its small nose leaf tends to make its snout resemble that of a pig.

The greater mouse-tailed bat depends entirely on insects for food and, in the cooler parts of its range, when insects are in short supply, it enters a deep, sleep-like state which is called torpor. While it is in this condition, it lives on the large fat store which is built up beforehand and may almost equal the bat's normal weight. Bodily functions, such as heart rate and temperature, fall to low levels during this period.

In early spring, these bats mate and about four months later the single offspring is born. It is suckled for about two months; sexual maturity is attained in its second year.

Suborder Microchiroptera - bats (almost 800 species)
Family/Species Rhinopomatidae - mouse-tailed bats (3 or 4 species)/Greater Mouse-tailed Bat *Rhinopoma microphyllum*
Length 12-16 cm (5-6.3 in)

Proboscis Bat

The proboscis bat gets its name from its somewhat extended snout but it is also characterized by having tufts of hair on its forearms. Its rather dull greyish-brown fur, with the paler-coloured lines on the back, probably affords it some camouflage when it is roosting by clinging to rocky crevices, rocks, or even man-made concrete structures, when it could be mistaken for a patch of lichen. It also has a short tail which projects through a hole in the tail membrane and it may be that this arrangement gives it greater manoeuvrability in the air. Members of this family are also known as sac-winged bats because of the glandular sacs which are found in the crooks of the elbows. These sacs produce a strongly smelling fluid, especially in the males, which may be used to attract females.

It lives in forested and scrubby areas close to water in the Central Americas from southern Mexico to Brazil. It feeds mainly on insects but, instead of hunting them near the tops of trees as many species do, it usually catches insects flying close to the surface of water. It may be that it has evolved this method of hunting because it is a slow flier and would be easy prey for hunting birds if it was flying at greater heights.

The single offspring is born between April and July and is usually hidden in some dark, safe place until it is old enough to look after itself at about the age of two months.

Suborder Microchiroptera - bats (almost 800 species)

Family/Species Emballonuridae - sheath-tailed bats (over 40 species)/Proboscis Bat *Rhynchonycteris naso*

Length 4.5-6.5 cm (1.8-2.5 in)

Two-lined Bat

The two-lined bat is a little longer than the proboscis bat, but it has a much greater wing span, and the glandular sacs in the crooks of the elbows are particularly well developed. It gets its name from its striking markings, particularly the two wavy lines which run the length of its back. It is thought that these lines may serve as camouflage by breaking up the outline of the animal, particularly when it is roosting. Each individual bat prefers to stick to one roosting site and will usually return to it after a night's foraging for insects.

Two-lined bats live in the lowland forests of Latin America from Mexico to Bolivia and Brazil. The single offspring is born during the rainy season.

Old World Sheath-tailed Bat

The Old World sheath-tailed bat inhabits the rain forests of parts of south-east Asia from Thailand to Malaysia, including Java, Sumatra, Borneo, and the Celebes. There they roost in small colonies of perhaps twelve individuals in cracks in rocks as well as caves within the forest. They all leave their roosting sights at the same time in the evening to fly in search of insects which they probably catch near the tops of the forest canopy. Like some of the other sheath-tailed bats, they may also eat some fruit or even flowers.

Little is known about the breeding biology of Old World sheath-tailed bats but it seems likely that they breed throughout the year and produce a single offspring.

Suborder Microchiroptera - bats (almost 800 species)
Family/Species Emballonuridae - sheath-tailed bats (over 40 species)/Two-lined Bat *Saccopteryx leptura*
Length 5-6 cm (2-2.4 in)

Suborder Microchiroptera - bats (almost 800 species)
Family/Species Emballonuridae - sheath-tailed bats (over 40 species)/ Old World Sheath-tailed Bat *Emballonura monticola*
Length 5-7 cm (2-2.8 in)

Tomb Bat

The tomb bat is found on the island of Madagascar eastwards on to the Asian mainland as far as southern Asia and has been depicted in 2000-year-old Chinese paintings. It lives in coconut groves and scrubby areas and is often found roosting in large colonies among the ruins of tombs and palaces - hence its rather frightening name which belies its appearance. It has a reddish-brown, somewhat shiny coat of short fur which is paler beneath.

It is a high flier and, after leaving its roosting sight at dusk, it will fly to heights of as much as 100 metres (330 feet) in search of its insect prey. Towards morning, they slowly descend. It is a very vocal animal and emits calls which even humans are able to hear.

Little seems to have been recorded about its breeding biology.

Suborder Microchiroptera - bats (almost 800 species)
Family/Species Emballonuridae - sheath-tailed bats (over 40 species)/Tomb Bat *Taphozous longimanus*
Length 8-9 cm (3-3.5 in)

White Bat

The white bat or ghost bat gets its name from the ghostly white coloration of its fur and even its wings. It lives in both forested areas and open land of Central America and Mexico where it feeds on insects. It seems odd that this nocturnal hunter has evolved the white colour which should serve to make it much more conspicuous in the dark. But, like its darker-coloured relatives, it appears to be just as effective in its hunting forays so its colour remains a mystery. It also differs from other members of the family in having no wing glands but there are sac-like glands in the tail membrane.

Like a number of other members of this family, it usually roosts alone in caves or crevices and cracks within rocks. Little is known of its breeding biology except that it probably breeds throughout the year.

Suborder Microchiroptera - bats (almost 800 species)
Family/Species Emballonuridae - sheath-tailed bats (over 40 species)/White Bat (Ghost Bat) *Diclidurus virgo*
Length 7-11 cm (2.8-4.3 in)

Hog-nosed Bat

Until the mid-1970s, this bat had not been described at all. It is also known as Kitti's hog-nosed bat or even the butterfly bat and, weighing a mere 2 grams, it is another contender for the place of the world's smallest bat. With most of its natural habitat destroyed, it now occupies the teak plantations and bamboo forests of Thailand, where it roosts in small colonies in limestone caves from which it emerges at dusk. It is thought to be extremely rare and in danger of extinction, but very little is known about it. It is possible that it may live in areas other than those in which it has so far been found.

It feeds on insects, and it may be that its pig-like nose, from which it gets one of its names, is an aid in picking its small prey from the surfaces of leaves. Its fur is brownish in colour and it has darker-brown wings. Nothing is known of its breeding biology.

Suborder Microchiroptera - bats (almost 800 species)
Family/Species Craseonycteridae - hog-nosed bats (1 species)/Hog-nosed Bat (Kitti's Hog-nosed Bat, Butterfly Bat) *Craseonycteris thonglongyai*
Length 3-3.5 cm (1.2-1.4 in)

Egyptian Slit-faced Bat

The Egyptian slit-faced bat inhabits the dry plains as well as the damp forests of the Middle East, Africa south of the Sahara Desert, and the island of Madagascar. Like other members of the family, it has a longitudinal furrow along the top of its snout which is covered by overlapping nose leaves. These structures are thought to be part of its echolocation system. Its tail, which extends to the end of the tail membrane, has a T-shaped bone at its tip which no other mammal has.

These bats roost, often singly, in caves and other places from which they emerge at dusk to feed on insects, spiders, scorpions, and other small invertebrates.

It is thought that there may be two periods every year in which young are born. A single young is born in January or February and there may be a second litter later in the year.

Suborder Microchiroptera - bats (almost 800 species)
Family/Species Nycteridae - slit-faced bats (10 species)/ Egyptian Slit-faced Bat *Nycteris thebaica*
Length 8-15 cm (3-6 in)

Greater False Vampire

The greater false vampire bat inhabits the forests as well as more open land from India to parts of south-east Asia, including Burma, southern China, and Malaysia. Some false vampire bats are purely insect eaters, which belies their name, but others supplement their diet with rodents, frogs, fishes, or even other bats. They sweep silently down on other bats and appear to chew their victim before devouring it which led to the idea that they were simply sucking their blood. In addition, to insects and vertebrates, the greater false vampire also eats spiders and other invertebrates.

Like all the false vampires, this species has long, upright ears and prominent, fluted nose leaves. They are greyish brown in colour which probably affords them some camouflage in the dark caves in which they roost. Other species of bats will not roost in caves occupied by small colonies of false vampires probably because of their predatory habits.

The single offspring is born in March after a gestation period of about five months.

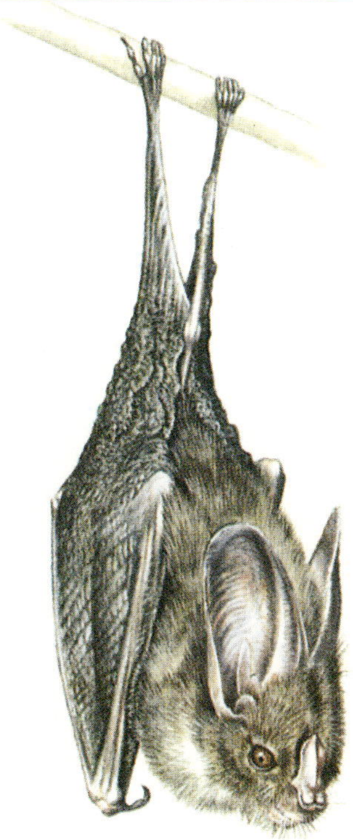

Suborder Microchiroptera - bats (almost 800 species)
Family/Species Megadermatidae - false vampires (5 species)/Greater False Vampire *Megaderma lyra*
Length 6.5-8.5 cm (2.6-3.3 in)

Heart-nosed Bat

The heart-nosed bat is found in forest and scrub lands of eastern central Africa from Ethiopia to Tanzania. It is similar in appearance, if rather paler coloured, than the greater false vampire but, as its name suggests, its nose leaves are wider and rather heart shaped.

Its way of life also resembles that of the other members of the family, and it feeds on a wide variety of invertebrates and vertebrates, including lizards. Indeed, in pursuit of wall lizards or rats and mice it will even fly into houses. It tends to emerge from its roost rather earlier than some other species. With its relatively long, broad wings, it is a strong flier and, unlike birds of prey, it can take off from the ground and become airborne carrying a load which is close to its own size. Like other members of this family, the heart-nosed bat preys upon other smaller bats, attacking them in the air by beating at them with its wings.

Suborder Microchiroptera - bats (almost 800 species)
Family/Species Megadermatidae - false vampires (5 species)/Heart-nosed Bat *Cardioderma cor*
Length 7-9 cm (2.75-3.5 in)

Australian False Vampire

Also known as the Australian ghost bat because of its generally pale coloration, the Australian false vampire is the largest of the microchiropteran bats and is now an endangered species. As its name suggests, it lives in forested areas of northern and western tropical Australia where it roosts in caves. It is long eared, with nose leaves typical of the family, and a tail membrane.

It is a highly predatory bat and feeds almost entirely on a diet of rodents, lizards, birds, and, of course, other bats. Dropping down upon its victim, it will trap the unfortunate creature in its powerful wings and then kill it by biting it in the back of the neck. It will then take to the air, carrying its prey, and return to a favourite perch in a tree or cave to eat.

Australian false vampires roost in colonies and the females are joined by the males in April. Each female gives birth to a single offspring in October or November just after the males have left the colony. Within three or four months, the young have reached adult size and join their mothers on hunting forays.

Suborder Microchiroptera - bats (almost 800 species)
Family/Species Megadermatidae - false vampires (5 species)/Australian False Vampire (Australian Ghost Bat) *Macroderma gigas*
Length 11.5-14 cm (4.5-5.5 in)

Yellow-winged Bat

The yellow-winged bat is found in Africa from Senegal to Kenya where it inhabits swampy land and forests or open country with lakes. With its variable but usually pale-coloured fur and yellowish wings and ears, the origin of its name is obvious. Like other members of the family, it has large ears and the nose leaves are the largest of all the group.

Although it has been seen flying during the day, it generally roosts among the foliage of trees where it is surprisingly hard to spot. Unlike other members of the family, it seems to eat mainly insects and behaves rather like a nocturnal flycatching bird. It will wait at a favourite perch from which it swoops on to a passing, unsuspecting insect, returning to its perch after snapping up its victim.

It is thought to breed throughout the year.

Suborder Microchiroptera - bats (almost 800 species)
Family/Species Megadermatidae - false vampires (5 species)/Yellow-winged Bat *Lavia frons*
Length 6.5-8 cm (2.6-3 in)

Greater Horseshoe Bat

The greater horseshoe bat inhabits forested, as well as open and cultivated land throughout Europe, North Africa, and Asia. All the members of this large family belong to the same genus. They get their name from the complicated arrangement of fleshy nose leaves consisting of a horseshoe-shaped rim around the nostrils; a fluted ridge arises between the nostrils and extends upwards as a pointed structure called a lancet. All of these structures seem to be aids in producing and directing the ultrasonic calls which are emitted through the nostrils with the mouth closed.

The greater horseshoe bat is a slow flier and, although its broad wings give it manoeuvrability in the air, it does not seem to be very good at catching insects in flight and usually prefers to swoop down and pounce on them on the ground. They roost in a variety of sites, but especially caves, potholes, or mine workings and, when they roost, they wrap their wings around their bodies instead of folding them as other bats do. During the winter months, they will hibernate in colonies of thousands, travelling long distances to find their favourite caves.

After the winter hibernation, the female bat gives birth to a single offspring in April which she suckles and carries with her for about three months. Many species of horseshoe bats are now endangered.

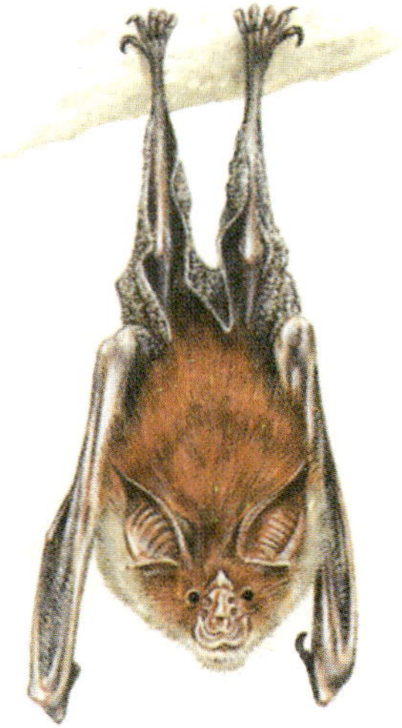

Suborder Microchiroptera - bats (almost 800 species)
Family/Species Rhinolophidae - horseshoe bats (50-70 species)/Greater Horseshoe Bat *Rhinolophus ferrumequinum*
Length 14-16 cm (5.5-6.3 in)

Lesser Horseshoe Bat

The lesser horseshoe bat has roughly the same range as its larger relative, from Europe to Asia, and including North Africa. It tends to live only in open country where there are caves in which it can hibernate in dry conditions although it may, of course, become very cold. It resembles the greater horseshoe bat in its appearance except that it has a slightly shorter body and tail, and a considerably smaller wing span. Through the summer months, it roosts during the day in trees, hollow logs, or even in houses where its presence becomes evident from its constant chattering calls.

It also feeds on insects but, although its flight is just as fluttering as that of the greater species, it seems to be still more manoeuvrable, and catches many more of its prey items on the wing.

Suborder Microchiroptera - bats (almost 800 species)
Family/Species Rhinolophidae - horseshoe bats (50-70 species)/Lesser Horseshoe Bat *Rhinolophus hipposideros*
Length 8.5-12.5 cm (3.5-5 in)

Philippine Horseshoe Bat

As its name suggests, the Philippine horseshoe bat is confined to the Philippine Islands off the coast of south-east Asia, where other bats are numerous in number and species. It inhabits broken country and primary forest.

Because of the competition from other bats, it has adapted to feeding on large, slow-flying insects and on ground-dwelling beetles. It is able to cut through the heavy armour of the beetles with its sharp teeth to get at the flesh.

It does not hibernate and it breeds throughout the year.

Persian Trident Bat

Although the Persian trident bat belongs to a different family to the horseshoe bats, the families are somewhat similar in appearance. The members of this family do have the horseshoe-shaped nose leaves although they are rather less well defined. Above its nose disc, this bat has curious prong-like structures from which it derives its name. They inhabit the arid and semidesert country of Egypt eastwards to Iran (formerly Persia).

They feed entirely on small insects for which they hunt among the high foliage. During the day, they roost in burrows, caves, cracks, and crevices in the ground and they emerge just before dusk to fly rapidly and at low level to their feeding areas.

A single offspring is born between December and May.

Suborder Microchiroptera - bats (almost 800 species)
Family/Species Rhinolophidae - horseshoe bats (50-70 species)/Philippine Horseshoe Bat *Rhinolophus philippinensis*
Length 8-11 cm (3-4.3 in)

Suborder Microchiroptera - bats (almost 800 species)
Family/Species Hipposideridae - Old World leaf-nosed bats (40-60 species)/Persian Trident Bat *Triaenops persicus*
Length 5-7 cm (2-2.8 in)

Flower-faced Bat

The flower-faced bat seems to be restricted to the Solomon Islands situated in the Pacific Ocean off the north-east coast of Australia. It is thought to inhabit forest and mixed agricultural land. Like many other members of this family, it is probably a drab greyish brown colour. Little is known about it, however, and only a few specimens have ever been collected.

It gets its name from the bizarre structures of its nose leaves. They are made up of layers which look rather like the arrangement of the petals of a flower but it is not known why it should possess such a complicated arrangement or what benefit it can possibly derive from it.

Suborder Microchiroptera - bats (almost 800 species)
Family/Species Hipposideridae - Old World leaf-nosed bats (40-60 species)/Flower-faced Bat *Anthops ornatus*
Length 5-6.5 cm (2-2.5 in)

Trident Leaf-nosed Bat

Like the Persian trident bat, the trident leaf-nosed bat gets its name from the three-pronged, lance-shaped structures above its nasal disc. Its orange-coloured fur contrasts markedly with the more drab coloration of most other members of this family. It has large, quite pointed ears with no fleshy prominences near the external openings.

Inhabiting dry, scrubby land from North Africa eastwards to India, it roosts in colonies of hundreds of individuals in underground tunnels or cracks. They emerge from their roosting sites in early evening to fly low over the ground to their feeding grounds among palm groves where they feed on the plentiful supply of insects which live in the damp and shady conditions there. Trident leaf-nosed bats seem to have an especial liking for moths and beetles.

Suborder Microchiroptera - bats (almost 800 species)
Family/Species Hipposideridae - Old World leaf-nosed bats (40-60 species)/Trident Leaf-nosed Bat *Asellia tridens*
Length 7-9 cm (2.8-3.5 in)

Large Malay Leaf-nosed Bat

The large Malay leaf-nosed bat is, as its name suggests, one of the larger members of this family, in which there is considerable size variation. It inhabits forested regions, often close to areas where people are living, in south-east Asia from Thailand eastwards to Malaysia - from which it derives another part of its name.

During the day it roosts in colonies of hundreds of individuals in caves or old buildings. At dusk, the bats emerge to search among flowers for their insect prey. They will even open fruit, such as figs, to get at the insect larvae hidden within.

A single offspring is born in November and December.

Tailless Leaf-nosed Bat

The tailless leaf-nosed bat inhabits the forests of the area which stretches from Bangladesh, in the north-east corner of the Indian subcontinent, through Indochina to Java in the east.

It is different in a number of respects from many of the other members of this family: its ears are shorter and more rounded; and, more especially, the structure of the nose leaves is far less complex.

During the day, these bats roost in groups of about twelve or more in hollow trees or in houses, but little seems to be known about their behaviour. In Java, at least, births have been observed to occur towards the end of February.

Suborder Microchiroptera - bats (almost 800 species)
Family/Species Hipposideridae - Old World leaf-nosed bats (40-60 species)/Large Malay Leaf-nosed Bat *Hipposideros diadema*
Length 10-13 cm (4-5 in)

Suborder Microchiroptera - bats (almost 800 species)
Family/Species Hipposideridae - Old World leaf-nosed bats (40-60 species)/Tailless Leaf-nosed Bat *Coelops frithi*
Length 4-6 cm (1.6-2.4 in)

Fisherman Bat

The family to which the fisherman bat belongs contains only two species and they are alternatively known as bulldog bats because of their characteristic vertical fold of skin below the nostrils, resembling a bulldog's muzzle. Both species inhabit swampy forests and mangrove swamps of Central and northern South America. The fisherman bat is found from Mexico south to Argentina, the Antilles, and the island of Trinidad.

As its name suggests, the fisherman bat eats fish as well as insects, which it catches in the air and on the water. The animal is particularly well adapted to its way of life. With its stiff-winged flight, it is a powerful flier, and it swoops down towards the water's surface and plucks out a fish using the very sharp claws with which its large feet are armed. The legs are very long and its orange-yellow fur seems to be able to shed water most effectively. Once the bat has scooped up the fish, it is transferred to its mouth where large morsels can be held in cheek pouches. It is known that they do use echolocation techniques and it is possible, therefore, that they locate their prey by detecting the ripples which a fish close to the surface would make.

The single offspring is born during February or March about four months after mating occurs during November or December.

Suborder Microchiroptera - bats (almost 800 species)
Family/Species Noctilionidae - fisherman bats (2 species)/Fisherman Bat *Noctilio leporinus*
Length 12-15 cm (4.7-6 in)

Moustached Bat

The moustached bat is one of eight species in its family which are also referred to as leaf-chinned bats. Once again, both these names originate from features which are characteristic of the group. They have a fringe of hairs which surrounds the mouth and, instead of a typical nose leaf, the upper and lower lips have developed to form a kind of dish shape. Some species of these comparatively short-eared bats appear to have naked backs because their wing membranes meet and join at the back. Both of these features are thought to aid in the capture of their insect prey.

The moustached bat inhabits lowland forests of Central and northern South America from northern Mexico to Brazil and including the West Indies. They are very gregarious animals and roost in caves in colonies which may number more than 500 000 individuals. As a consequence, their droppings accumulate on the floors of the caves and the guano is collected for use as fertilizer. Unlike most bats, which hang vertically when roosting, moustached bats lie horizontally. The females give birth to a single offspring each year in May.

Suborder Microchiroptera - bats (almost 800 species)
Family/Species Mormoopidae - moustached or leaf-chinned bats (8 species)/Moustached Bat *Pteronotus parnelli*
Length 5.5-10.5 cm (2.2-4 in)

Leaf-chinned Bat

The leaf-chinned bat inhabits forested and scrubby land, often close to water, from Arizona in the United States south to northern South America and including the island of Trinidad in the West Indies. It has reddish-coloured fur but it is distinguished from the other members of the family more by the pair of fleshy, leaf-like flaps on its chin and distinct, peg-like growths on the lower lip.

During the day, leaf-chinned bats roost in caves and tunnels as well as in cracks and fissures in rocks. They emerge from their roost sites after dark to hunt for their insect food, and indeed, they take to the wing later than most other species of bats. They fly quite low and often search for their prey over the pools and swamps of the regions in which they live.

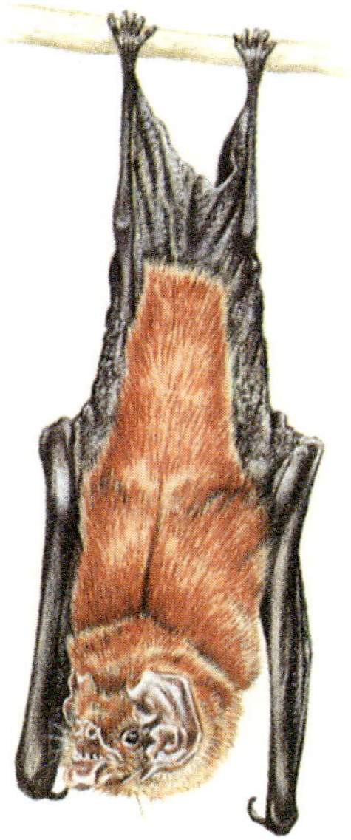

Suborder Microchiroptera - bats (almost 800 species)
Family/Species Mormoopidae - moustached or leaf-chinned bats (8 species)/Leaf-chinned Bat *Mormoops megalophylla*
Length 8.5-9 cm (3.3-3.5 in)

Vampire Bat

There are three species of vampire bat in this family, living in the forested regions of Central and South America from Mexico to Argentina. The vampire bat itself ranges from northern Mexico to central Chile, Argentina, and Uruguay. It is not entirely surprising that the mythical stories of the living dead feeding upon the blood of other humans have become linked with vampire bats: these mammals fly during the darkest time of the night and feed exclusively on the blood of other mammals and birds.

The vampire bat feeds mainly on the blood of domestic cattle. It flies in close to its host and then crawls along the ground to approach it. It finds a part of the animal's body which is not protected by hair and then makes a small incision with its four razor-sharp incisor teeth. To prevent the animal's blood from clotting, the bat pumps saliva into the wound and then uses its tongue to lap up the blood. The tongue itself is grooved and forms a tube-like structure although the bat does not actually suck the blood of its host. Each bat feeds only for about thirty minutes before it is satisfied and the amount of blood lost by its host is relatively small. Unfortunately, however, the bats may themselves carry diseases, such as rabies, which may be transmitted to the victim. These bats may truly be described as parasites and, indeed, they are the only mammals which behave in this way. It is, therefore, not in the interests of the bat to cause its host any serious damage or to kill it by its attentions. But, of course, if a number of bats feed on the same animal it may become seriously weakened.

Suborder Microchiroptera - bats (almost 800 species)
Family/Species Desmodontidae - vampire bats (3 species)/Vampire Bat *Desmodus rotundus*
Length 7.5-9 cm (3-3.5 in)

Egyptian Free-tailed Bat

The Egyptian free-tailed bat inhabits dry scrubby land of North Africa and the Middle East although other members of this large family range right across the warmer and tropical parts of the Old and New Worlds from the central Americas, through southern Europe, parts of Asia, and into Australasia. They feed exclusively on insects which are caught in flight, their long, narrow wings enabling them to fly more quickly than many other species of bats. They get their name from the relatively long, thick, rat-like tail which extends beyond the tail membrane.

During the day, they roost, in colonies of thousands of individuals, in a variety of sites from caves, to crevices, and even trees and buildings. About two to three months after the mating period in winter a single offspring is born and the female may mate again almost immediately.

Velvety Free-tailed Bat

Found in Central America, northern South America, and the Caribbean islands, this bat gets its name from the velvety, short, dense, dark-brown fur. It also has a rat-like tail which projects beyond the tail membrane but, in relation to the length of its body, it is a little shorter than that of the Egyptian species.

Like the other members of this group, it feeds on insects. It has large cheek pouches which it crams with insects before returning to its roost to eat them. In this way, it shortens the time spent hunting and is less likely to be a meal for some other predator.

The young are born in summer.

Suborder Microchiroptera - bats (almost 800 species)
Family/Species Molossidae - free-tailed bats (over 80 species)/Egyptian Free-tailed Bat *Tadarida aegyptiaca*
Length 8-12 cm (3-4.7 in)

Suborder Microchiroptera - bats (almost 800 species)
Family/Species Molossidae - free-tailed bats (over 80 species)/Velvety Free-tailed Bat *Molossus ater*
Length 9-13 cm (3.5-5 in)

Wroughton's Free-tailed Bat

Wroughton's free-tailed bat occupies the open and partly forested country of southern India and the island of Sri Lanka. Little is known about this species and only a few specimens have ever been collected so that it may appear to be a rare member of the family. Other species within the group, however, may be the most common mammals within their range and it may be that this bat is more common than it seems. To add to its apparent rarity, during the day, it roosts either singly or in small groups. Like other members of the free-tailed bat family, this species has no need to hibernate owing to the favourable climate in the areas where it lives.

The single offspring is born in December.

Suborder Microchiroptera - bats (almost 800 species)
Family/Species Molossidae - free-tailed bats (over 80 species)/Wroughton's Free-tailed Bat *Otomops wroughtoni*
Length 12.5-16 cm (5-6.3 in)

Mastiff Bat

The forest-dwelling mastiff bat is often found close to human habitations in the south-western United States, Mexico, and southwards to the northern parts of South America. It is greyish in colour with a pinkish snout and large, pink ears. Its rat-like tail may be more than half the length of its body.

After dark, mastiff bats fly from their roosting sites in rock fissures and buildings to hunt small, usually social insects, such as ants, wasps, and bees. They are reluctant fliers but move on the ground with considerable agility. The male mastiff bat has a gland in its throat which swells considerably when they are ready to mate. These glands secrete strong-smelling substances which may serve to attract receptive females. Usually the single offspring is born in late summer although, in some cases, the female may give birth to twins.

Suborder Microchiroptera - bats (almost 800 species)
Family/Species Molossidae - free-tailed bats (over 80 species)/Mastiff Bat *Eumops perotis*
Length 10-14 cm (4-5.5 in)

Long-tongued Bat

The long-tongued bat belongs to a large family of bats, most of which have a nose leaf above the nostrils. In many cases, this flap of tissue may be somewhat pointed giving the family its alternative name of spear-nosed bats. The long-tongued bat inhabits dry woodland from northern Mexico to Brazil, Paraguay, and Argentina as well as the West Indies. It has a pointed snout and a long, narrow, bristly tongue which can be extended.

Hovering in front of a bloom, rather like a hummingbird, it scoops up nectar using its tongue. It may also eat the juice of ripe fruit as well as insects.

Usually a single young is born in summer.

American False Vampire

Like the false vampires of the Old World, it was once thought that this animal sucked the blood of its victims. It is now known to be predatory, killing and eating rats, mice, birds, and even other bats. Although it is one of the largest New World bats, it is quite agile on the ground and can creep up on its prey before pouncing on it and either smashing its skull or breaking its neck. It is found from southern Mexico to Peru and Brazil as well as on the West Indian island of Trinidad; it inhabits forests often quite close to where humans are living.

The single offspring is born in June and the mother is very attentive to its young.

Suborder Microchiroptera - bats (almost 800 species)
Family/Species Phyllostomatidae - New World leaf-nosed bats (about 140 species)/Long-tongued Bat (Spear-nosed Long-tongued Bat) *Glossophaga soricina*
Length 5.5-7 cm (2.2-2.8 in)

Suborder Microchiroptera - bats (almost 800 species)
Family/Species Phyllostomatidae - New World leaf-nosed bats (about 140 species)/American False Vampire *Vampyrum spectrum*
Length 17.5-19 cm (7-7.5 in)

Tent-building Bat

Unlike other members of this family, which usually roost in caves, mines, animal burrows, and so on, the tent-building bat builds its own daytime shelter, as its name suggests. Living, as it does, in the forests and plantations from southern Mexico to Peru and Brazil, as well as Trinidad, it has plenty of raw material from which to construct its 'tent'. It bites partially through the leaf ribs of a fan-shaped palm leaf about a third of the way along it. The leaf bends to form the tent-like shelter which may be shared by a small colony of twenty or thirty animals. The bats fly out to feed on ripe fruit.

The fur of the tent-building bat is a brownish colour, like that of many other members of the family, and it also has a pair of white lines running along the top of its head as well as a pale stripe on its back. This bat has no tail, somewhat pointed ears, and a spear-shaped nose leaf.

The leaf tents are also used as nurseries by groups of nursing, with which the young stay until they are able to fly. During this time, the males live alone or in small, all-male groups, returning to the females only after the young have finished suckling. The offspring are born between February and April. Like most other mammals living in essentially tropical regions, these bats do not hibernate.

Suborder Microchiroptera - bats (almost 800 species)
Family/Species Phyllostomatidae - New World leaf-nosed bats (about 140 species)/Tent-building Bat *Uroderma bilobatum*
Length 5.5-7.5 cm (2.2-3 in)

Spear-nosed Bat

The spear-nosed bat has, as its name implies, a particularly well-developed spear-shaped nose leaf above its nostrils, a characteristic feature of the family. It is one of the larger bats which lives in the Americas although another member of the family, the false vampire which has already been described, is America's biggest bat. The spear-nosed bat lives in the central parts of the Americas from Belize to Peru, Bolivia, and Brazil as well as the West Indian island of Trinidad where it inhabits forest and other types of broken country.

Although most other bats of this family eat insects, with some feeding on fruit, pollen, and nectar, the spear-nosed bat has a diet of meat rather like that of the false vampire. It feeds mainly on birds, other bats, and small rodents although it supplements its diet with insects and even fruit. During the day, they roost in huge colonies in caves and unoccupied buildings from which they emerge at dusk to fly to their feeding grounds.

The offspring are born during the months of May and June in the colonial roosting site.

Suborder Microchiroptera - bats (almost 800 species)
Family/Species Phyllostomatidae - New World leaf-nosed bats (about 140 species)/Spear-nosed Bat *Phyllostomus hastatus*
Length 12.5-15.5 cm (5-6 in)

Yellow-shouldered Bat

The yellow-shouldered bat gets its name from the tufts of yellowish fur on its shoulders. It is tailless and has only a very narrow band of tail membrane between its hind limbs. It inhabits the lowland forests of the central Americas from northern Mexico to Paraguay and Argentina as well as on the West Indian island of Jamaica.

It is another fruit eater and it roosts either singly or in small colonies in deserted buildings, hollow trees, or in the top parts of palm trees.

It does not hibernate in any part of its range although its breeding behaviour differs from region to region. In the north, breeding occurs throughout the year while, in the southern part of the bat's range, the female gives birth to its single offspring between May and July.

Short-tailed Leaf-nosed Bat

The short-tailed leaf-nosed bat is, once again, found in the central parts of America from southern Mexico to southern Brazil where it lives in forests and plantations. As its name suggests, its tail is short and does not project beyond the tail membrane. The fur is a medium-brown colour.

Probably finding its food by smell, this member of the leaf-nosed bat family eats mainly ripe fruit, such as bananas, figs, guavas, and plantains.

It breeds throughout the year with the female giving birth to a single offspring.

Suborder Microchiroptera - bats (almost 800 species)
Family/Species Phyllostomatidae - New World leaf-nosed bats (about 140 species)/Yellow-shouldered Bat *Sturnira lilium*
Length 6-7 cm (2.4-2.8 in)

Suborder Microchiroptera - bats (almost 800 species)
Family/Species Phyllostomatidae - New World leaf-nosed bats (about 140 species)/Short-tailed leaf-nosed Bat *Carollia perspicillata*
Length 5.5-8 cm (2.2-3 in)

Little Big-eared Bat

The little big-eared bat seems to be quite adaptable in its choice of habitat occupying country from dry scrubland to tropical rain forest. It ranges from the south-western parts of the United States to Peru and Brazil in South America, as well as the islands of Trinidad, Tobago, and Grenada. Its name is very apt in that, in relation to the size of its head and body, its ears do appear to be particularly large. It has a short tail which does not protrude beyond the tail membrane. Its fur is a foxy brown with pale parts on its cheeks and undersides.

Little big-eared bats seem to be omnivorous and feed on both insects and fruit. Among their insect prey, which are hunted in flight and on the ground, they seem to prefer heavy, slow-flying insects, such as cockchafers, as well as cockroaches. Thus, like many species of bats, they help to control certain insect pests and perform a valuable service to humankind.

With the onset of dusk they fly out of their roosting sites and hunt by flying around fruit trees. During the day they roost in small groups in a variety of holes.

In April and May the females give birth usually to a single offspring.

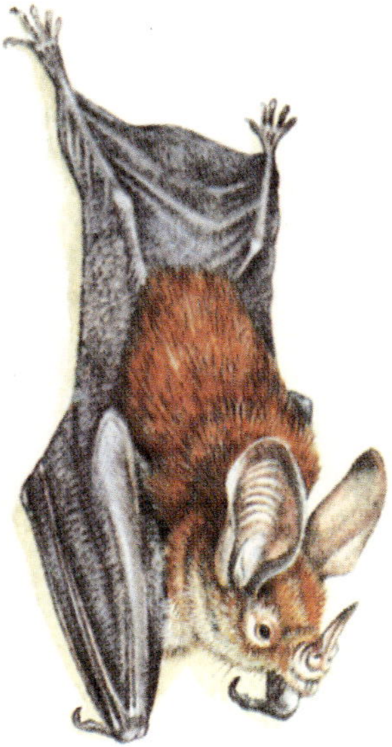

Suborder Microchiroptera - bats (almost 800 species)
Family/Species Phyllostomatidae - New World leaf-nosed bats (about 140 species)/Little Big-eared Bat *Micronycteris megalotis*
Length 4.5-7.5 cm (1.8-3 in)

Jamaican Fruit-eating Bat

Although its name implies that it is confined to the West Indian island of Jamaica, this tailless bat is, in fact, found in the Central American mainland from northern Mexico to Brazil and northern Argentina as well as on the West Indies. In these areas, it inhabits scrubland as well as forest, living exclusively on a diet of fruit. Indeed, it seems to be able to digest its food so quickly that the fruit seeds pass through its gut undamaged. Consequently, it is of considerable value to the plants on whose fruit it feeds because it aids in the distribution of their seeds.

At any time between February and July one or possibly two offspring are born to each breeding female.

Cuban Flower Bat

Most bats of this family are darkly coloured in greys, browns, and black. The Cuban flower bat, however, has a very pale grey coat. It does not possess the spear-shaped nose leaf which is typical of the family. Its name is very descriptive because it is confined to the island of Cuba and it does feed on the nectar and pollen of a wide variety of flowers using its long, slender tongue. Its also feeds on fruit, however, in its habitat of cultivated land and primary forest.

It is a very social animal and roosts in caves in colonies of hundreds or even thousands of individuals. Breeding takes place all year and the young stay at the roost until they can fly.

Suborder Microchiroptera - bats (almost 800 species)
Family/Species Phyllostomatidae - New World leaf-nosed bats (about 140 species)/Jamaican Fruit-eating Bat *Artibeus jamaicensis*
Length 7.5-9 cm (3-3.5 in)

Suborder Microchiroptera - bats (almost 800 species)
Family/Species Phyllostomatidae - New World leaf-nosed bats (about 140 species)/Cuban Flower Bat *Phyllonycteris poeyi*
Length 8.5-9.5 cm (3.3-3.7 in)

Little Brown Bat

The little brown bat belongs to the evening or common bat family which probably contains at least 300 species and is distributed throughout the world except for the polar regions. Indeed, the genus *Myotis*, comprising the sixty or so different species of little brown bats, may be the mostly widely distributed of all mammalian genera, with the single exception of humans. This species is found throughout North America from Canada through the United States to Mexico in the south; it is very common, inhabiting forested and built-up areas. Bearing in mind the extent of its range, it is clearly able to survive in widely differing climates although those living in the northern regions hibernate to withstand the rigours of winter, often flying hundreds of kilometres to find suitable hibernation sites.

It has widely separated ears and a long tail to support the broad tail membrane which may be well over half the length of its body. Like most members of the family, the little brown bat feeds on insects which it pinpoints by the echolocation system that it also uses to navigate.

Breeding takes place during the summer and, following mating, the females gather together in maternity roosting sites to give birth to their young after a gestation period of a couple of months. Usually a single offspring is born although twins are not uncommon; the young reach breeding maturity when they are about a year old.

Suborder Microchiroptera - bats (almost 800 species)
Family/Species Vespertilionidae - evening bats (at least 300 species)/Little Brown Bat *Myotis lucifugus*
Length 6.5 cm (2.6 in)

Fish-eating Bat

The fish-eating bat is a coastal-dwelling species, relying, as it does on a diet of marine fishes and crustaceans. It is found on the western seaboard of America from California to Mexico where it roosts in caves and among rock piles. This bat is particularly well adapted to catch its slippery prey. It has long legs with long, sharply clawed toes and, in late evening, it skims over the surface of the sea, plucking its victims from the water with its feet.

The single offspring is born in May or June and the mother carries it with her on flights until it is half grown when it remains in the roost.

Common Long-eared Bat

As its name suggests, the common long-eared bat's ears are enormous and may be as much as 75 per cent of the length of the body. There is a prominent projection (tragus) at the base of each ear opening. The common long-eared bat also has a very long tail. It is found across northern Europe through Asia as far as north-eastern China and into Japan where it lives in sheltered, lightly wooded areas.

They emerge from their roosting sites in trees and buildings at dusk to feed on night-flying insects.

The single offspring is born in June in maternity roosts containing females and their young only. Hibernation begins in mid-November and may last until early April.

Suborder Microchiroptera - bats (almost 800 species)
Family/Species Vespertilionidae - evening bats (at least 300 species)/Fish-eating Bat *Pizonyx vivesi*
Length 12-15 cm (4.7-6 in)

Suborder Microchiroptera - bats (almost 800 species)
Family/Species Vespertilionidae - evening bats (at least 300 species)/Common Long-eared Bat *Plecotus auritus*
Length 7-9.5 cm (2.8-3.7 in)

Common Pipistrelle

Often popularly known as the 'flying mouse', the common pipistrelle inhabits open country throughout Europe and as far east as Kashmir. It is probably Europe's commonest bat and is relatively small with short ears and small, wide-set eyes. Living in the cool climates of temperate regions, these bats must hibernate to survive the winter cold when their food is hard to find. They usually migrate to a suitably dry cave where they will pass the cold months in huge colonies of 100 000 individuals or more. At other times of the year, however, they will roost in a variety of sites, including the lofts of houses, church spires, and farm buildings where they will still gather in very large numbers. They emerge at dusk to hunt insects; small items are eaten in flight but larger insects are usually taken to a convenient perch to be devoured.

Pipistrelles mate in September, before hibernation, but there is delayed implantation so that the sperm of the male is stored by the female for seven or eight months before fertilization actually takes place and the embryo begins to develop. The actual gestation period lasts for about two months and the offspring are born in June. Usually, the female gives birth to a single young but twins are not unknown. Females segregate from the males to form nursing colonies before the young are born.

Suborder Microchiroptera - bats (almost 800 species)
Family/Species Vespertilionidae - evening bats (at least 300 species)/Common Pipistrelle *Pipistrellus pipistrellus*
Length 5.5-7.5 cm (2.16-3 in)

Big Brown Bat

Despite its common name, the big brown bat belongs to a different genus to the little brown bat. It is larger, however, and is similar in overall appearance. Its wingspan may be almost twice that of the smaller species and it has a much longer tail which is contained within the tail membrane. It is found in the Americas from Alaska in the north to Central America in the south and including the islands of the West Indies in the Caribbean.

Big brown bats are fast fliers and capture all kinds of insects, including water beetles, although they do not seem to prey upon moths which are often the staple diet of other species, such as the common long-eared bat. Like a number of other mammals dwelling in temperate regions, they hibernate during the winter and, in the southern United States, vast numbers may migrate to dry caves for the purpose. They will, however, hibernate in houses.

In summer, females gather in segregated nursing colonies to give birth and to rear their young. West of the Rocky Mountains, a single offspring is usual but, in the eastern parts of their range, twins are often born.

Suborder Microchiroptera - bats (almost 800 species)
Family/Species Vespertilionidae - evening bats (at least 300 species)/Big Brown Bat *Eptesicus fuscus*
Length 9.5-13 cm (3.7-5 in)

Red Bat

The red bat is found throughout North America and on the islands of the West Indies. Perhaps rather surprisingly, they have also colonized the Galapagos Islands in the Pacific Ocean off the west coast of Ecuador. They prefer to inhabit forested country where there are some open areas. Unlike most other members of this family which are generally coloured dull greys and browns, the red bat's coat, as its name implies, varies from a rusty shade to brick red and it is also overspread with white.

The red bat is most unusual in at least two of its characteristics. Unlike most bats, which usually give birth to one or occasionally two offspring in each litter, this species produces three or even sometimes four young at a time. The mother carries her offspring with her at first, even though the combined weight of the litter may exceed her own bodyweight - this is good evidence of their powers of flight!

Red bats living in colder regions migrate southwards in autumn and north again in spring. They hibernate, however, to survive the rigours of winter and, during this period, the animal's internal body temperature falls to as low as -5 degrees centigrade (23 degrees Fahrenheit) which is the lowest recorded for any species of bat.

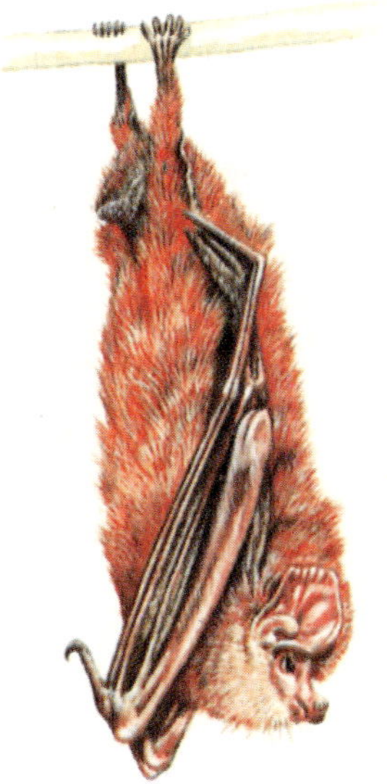

Suborder Microchiroptera - bats (almost 800 species)
Family/Species Vespertilionidae - evening bats (at least 300 species)/Red Bat *Lasiurus borealis*
Length 10.5-13 cm (4-5 in)

Noctule Bat

The noctule is found throughout Europe and central Asia, as far east as Japan, although it seems to be absent from Ireland. With its large size and reddish-brown fur, it is a distinctive-looking bat which, throughout its range, could hardly be confused with any other species with the possible exception of the rare greater noctule. The noctule prefers mainly forested country although it does fly over more open land to feed and may roost in isolated trees. It eats mainly insects, such as cockchafers (maybugs), crickets, and the common European dungbeetle although it has been suggested that it might even hunt mice. Emerging in the early evening, it will fly at considerable heights in search of its prey, and has even been seen with birds such as swifts and swallows.

Hollow trees are the favoured roosting sites, and loud squeaks often indicate the presence of a noctule colony, especially in summer, when the females segregate to form nusring groups. During the cold winter months, when food is scarce, they hibernate in mixed groups of up to 1000 individuals. Those living in more northerly regions migrate southwards to hibernate.

Mating takes place during the autumn and winter but implantayion is delayed until spring. Usually one, but sometimes two, offspring are born in June or July after a gestation period of about seventy days.

Suborder Microchiroptera - bats (almost 800 species)
Family/Species Vespertilionidae - evening bats (at least 300 species)/Noctule Bat (Noctule) *Nyctalus noctula*
Length 10-15.5 cm (4-6 in)

Barbastelle

At close quarters, the barbastelle is very distinctive. It has dark greyish-brown fur and relatively short, black ears which meet across the top of its head. It is also characterized by its short muzzle. They are found throughout most of central Europe as far east as central Russia. They have a patchy distribution in Britain but they also occur in North Africa. They inhabit open or lightly wooded country, often near water.

During the summer months they are hard to find; they roost during the day in holes and crevices in trees, emerging, often before sunset, to hunt for insects which they catch as they swoop low over water and bushes. During the winter, barbastelles may be found hibernating in deep, dry, limestone caves in numbers of up to 2000 individuals.

The breeding season occurs in the summer when the males and females separate, the latter to gather in maternity groups to give birth to their young.

Suborder Microchiroptera - bats (almost 800 species)
Family/Species Vespertilionidae - evening bats (at least 300 species/Barbastelle *Barbastella barbastellus*
Length 8-9.5 cm (3-3.7 in)

Painted Bat

Seen in isolation, the coloration of the painted bat is most striking. Its fur is reddish or orange while the wing membrane is black and the bones of its digits are highlighted in orange. It is not hard to see the origins of its name. It is, however, more difficult to believe that this bright patterning may help to camouflage the animal when it is roosting in small groups. However, the bold patterning probably serves to break up its outline and make it harder to spot in the unlikely sites which it chooses among foliage and flowers, in old weaverbird nests, or under the eaves of habitations. Its tail may be as long as its body.

It inhabits the dry woodland of southern Africa including southern Kenya, Namibia, and Natal province of South Africa.

Nothing is known about the breeding biology of this bat.

Suborder Microchiroptera - bats (almost 800 species)
Family/Species Vespertilionidae - evening bats (at least 300 species)/Painted Bat *Kerivoula argentata*
Length 6-11 cm (2.4-4.3)

Mexican Funnel-eared Bat

Little is known about these bats, and even the number of species in the family to which it belongs is questionable. Obviously, they get their name from the large, funnel-shaped ears. They are all lightly built, rather small animals with long, narrow wings and long legs which give the family its alternative name of long-legged bats. The tails, which are often longer than the body, are contained within the tail membrane. The males resemble the females except that they have glandular pads on their muzzles, although their function is unknown.

Mexican funnel-eared bats occur in the tropical lowlands of the central Americas from northern Mexico to Brazil and including the Lesser Antilles which is an archipelago of small islands in the Caribbean. They roost in caves, either in large colonies or small groups, from which they emerge at dusk to go in search of small, slow-flying insects which they pinpoint by echolocation. Their own flight is rather fluttering and moth-like.

They probably breed throughout the year with the females forming maternity colonies just before they give birth to their offspring.

Suborder Microchiroptera - bats (almost 800 species)
Family/Species Natalidae - funnel-eared bats (at least 3 species)/Mexican Funnel-eared Bat *Natalus stramineus*
Length 8-11.5 cm (3-4.5 in)

Smoky Bat

Little is known about the two species of Central American, forest-dwelling smoky bats which belong to this family. They are both a smoky grey or brown in colour, and one curious feature is that the thumbs are reduced to a tiny claw with no function. As a consequence, the bats must perform a somersault in the air to gain a foothold on the roofs of the caves or tunnels in which they have been found to roost. They also have very long tails contained within the tail membrane and the broad, funnel-shaped ears almost cover the eyes. The muzzle is set square against the high forehead. Their diet consists of insects.

Honduran Disc-winged Bat

Despite its name, the Honduran disc-winged bat inhabits the forests of Central and South America from Belize south to Ecuador and Peru. It gets its name from the stalked, sucker-like discs at the base of each thumb, and on the ankles, which help them to climb up the smooth branches and trunks of the trees of their forest home; these bats are even able to climb up a sheet of glass.

They roost in the young, curled leaves of large-leaved plants and they must search for a new site each day. They emerge to hunt for the insects on which they feed.

Breeding takes place throughout the year and the single offspring is carried by its mother until it weighs almost half as much as she does.

Suborder Microchiroptera - bats (almost 800 species)
Family/Species Furipteridae - smoky bats (2 species)/Smoky Bat *Furipterus horrens*
Length 8-12 cm (3-4.7 in)

Suborder Microchiroptera - bats (almost 800 species)
Family/Species Thyropteridae - disc-winged bats (2 species)/Honduran Disc-winged Bat *Thyroptera discifera*
Length 5.5-8 cm (2.2-3 cm)

Sucker-footed Bat

The sucker-footed bat, which is the sole representative of its family, is found only on the island of Madagascar off the east coast of Africa in the Indian Ocean. It has suction pads at the base of the thumbs and on the ankles but they are not connected by stalks as they are in the disc-winged bats, although they probably serve the same function - if less effectively. They roost inside the curled leaves of plants, as well as in hollow plant stems and occasionally on tree trunks.

Nothing is known about the breeding habits of this species nor about their diet. It seems likely, however, that they are becoming increasingly rare as their forest habitat is cut down.

New Zealand Short-tailed Bat

This bat inhabits the forests of New Zealand where it scurries with considerable agility among the leaf litter on the forest floor in search of insects. It is remarkably well adapted to walking and climbing: the wings fold so compactly that the forelimbs can be used as legs, aided by the long-clawed toes; the sturdy feet also bear talons. The animal also has a moustache-like fringe of hairs surrounding its mouth.

Unlike the other species of New Zealand bat, the short-tailed bat does not hibernate. It roosts, however, in small colonies in hollow trees. The female gives birth to a single offspring in October.

Suborder Microchiroptera - bats (almost 800 species)
Family/Species Myzopodidae - sucker-footed bats (1 species)/Sucker-footed Bat *Myzopoda aurita*
Length 9.5-11 cm (3.7-4.3 in)

Suborder Microchiroptera - bats (almost 800 species)
Family/Species Mystacinidae - short-tailed bats (1 or 2 species)/New Zealand Short-tailed Bat *Mystacina tuberculata*
Length 6.5-8 cm (2.6-3.2 in)

Glossary

altruistic behaviour behaviour which benefits another individual without necessarily benefiting the individual behaving altruistically.

amphibian any of the vertebrate animals of the class Amphibia, including frogs, toads, and newts, which are able to survive on land in damp places but which must return to the water to breed.

anatomy the structure and organization of the body of an animal or plant.

carnivore an animal or plant which feeds mainly on the flesh of other animals.

cartilage the tough, flexible tissue, otherwise known as gristle, of which the skeleton of certain fishes, such as sharks, is made. It also occurs in the joints of other vertebrates.

convergent evolution the process in which completely unrelated animals or plants evolve similar structures as a result of living in similar environmental conditions or having similar life styles. For example, insects, birds, and bats have all developed wings and carry out powered flight.

delayed implantation the process in which the fertilized egg lies dormant for some period of time in the womb of certain animals, such as seals or badgers, so that birth will occur at the most favourable time following a normal period of development without the offspring growing to too large a size for birth to occur.

echolocation the method by which animals, such as whales or bats, pinpoint objects by transmitting and receiving usually high-pitched sounds. These are reflected by objects in the vicinity and the time taken for the sound to return, its frequency, and direction enable the animal to locate its quarry as well as its speed and direction of motion with great accuracy.

ecology the study or science of the relationships between plants, animals, and their environment.

evolution the process in which, over long periods of time, populations of animals and plants change gradually as environmental conditions alter. Individuals which are well adapted tend to breed with greatest success and thereby contribute most to successive generations. Ultimately, new species will emerge and poorly adapted ones will become extinct.

gestation period in breeding, the period of time which elapses between conception and the birth of the offspring.

guano a natural fertilizer made up of the accumulated droppings of, particularly, seabirds or bats.

habitat an area within which an animal or plant lives where, at any particular time, the conditions of the environment are uniform.

herbivore an animal which feeds largely on plant material.

hibernation the resting state in which certain bats and other mammals survive long periods of cold weather and food shortage. Vital body functions, such as heart rate, are reduced and body temperature is lowered.

homoiothermic describing an animal which maintains its internal body temperature at a roughly constant level despite changing external temperatures.

invertebrate any animal lacking a backbone.

lancet any pointed structure such as that which forms part of the nasal structures of certain bats

larynx a cartilaginous structure at the top of the windpipe in terrestrial vertebrates which closes to prevent food entering the windpipe when the animal is eating.

mammal any animal of the class Mammalia, such as a dog or a whale. Mammals have backbones, are usually covered with a coat of hair to insulate them because they are poikilothermic, and feed their offspring through the early part of life on milk secreted by the mother's mammary glands.

mammary gland any of the glands on a female mammal which secrete milk to feed a developing offspring during the early part of its life.

New World that part of the world which comprises the Americas.

nocturnal active by night

Old World that part of the world which comprises Europe, Asia, and Africa.

omnivore any animal which eats both animal and plant material.

parasite any organism which benefits at the expense of another; for example, the vampire bat feeds on the blood of other mammals.

pelvis that part of the skeleton of an animal to which the bones of the hind limbs are attached.

physiology the study of the way in which animals or plants function.

poikilothermic describing an animal whose internal body temperature varies in response to changing external conditions.

pollinator any agent, such as the wind, an insect, or a bat, which transfers pollen from one flower to another.

polyandry the condition in which females mate with more than one male in the same breeding season.

predator any organism which hunts and kills other animals for food.

reptile any of the vertebrate animals, such as snakes and lizards, which belong to the class Reptilia. They lay eggs and are fully adapted to life on land.

sweat gland any of the small glands in the skin of a mammal which will exude sweat to enable the animal to cool itself by evaporation.

roosting the process in which animals, such as birds or bats, settle on a convenient, safe perch to pass the hours during which they are not active.

taxonomy the science of classification of living things.

temperate describing those parts of the world, between the tropics and the poles, where the climate is not extreme.

terrestrial describing an animal or plant which lives or grows on land.

torpor a resting state in which the activity of certain vital bodily functions is reduced to conserve energy. Certain animals become torpid during adverse weather conditions.

tropical describing that part of the world, immediately north and south of the equator, in which the conditions are generally warm and humid throughout the year.

vertebrate any of the animals which are included in the subphylum Vertebrata, such as fishes, amphibians, reptiles, birds, and mammals, and which are characterized by having a backbone throughout their adult lives.

Further reading

Macdonald, Dr David (ed.). *The Encyclopedia of Mammals*, Vol. 2. George Allen & Unwin, London, 1984.

Yalden, D W and Morris, P A. *The Lives of Bats*. David & Charles, Newton Abbot, 1975.

INDEX

Numbers in *italics* refer to illustrations